Ahalya
(A long poem)

Ahalya

(A long poem)

Phani Mohanty

Translated by
Sonali Sahu

BLACK EAGLE BOOKS
Dublin, USA | BBSR, India

 Black Eagle Books
USA address:
7464 Wisdom Lane
Dublin, OH 43016

India address:
E/312, Trident Galaxy, Kalinga Nagar,
Bhubaneswar-751003, Odisha, India

E-mail: info@blackeaglebooks.org
Website: www.blackeaglebooks.org

First International Edition Published by
Black Eagle Books, 2025

AHALYA (A long poem)
by **Phani Mohanty**
Translated by **Sonali Sahu**

Original Copyright © Phani Mohanty
Translation Copyright © Sonali Sahu

All rights reserved. No part of this publication may be reproduced, stored in a retrieval system, or transmitted, in any form or by any means, electronic, mechanical, photocopying, recording or otherwise without the prior permission of the publisher.

Cover design: **GK Padhi**
Interior Design: Ezy's Publication

ISBN- 978-1-64560-681-9 (Paperback)

Printed in the United States of America

I dedicate this work to
Goddess Sri Radha,
for being my eternal source of strength,
grace, and wisdom
throughout my literary journey.

Preface

"Ars longa, vita brevis"- this timeless Latin aphorism reminds us of the enduring nature of art in the face of life's fleeting brevity. In this context, poetry becomes a unique manifestation of human expression, an art form that transcends the limitations of time. It is through poetry that the human heart and mind connect with something greater than ordinary existence, reaching into the depths of human experience, emotion and understanding. Poetry, when it resonates melodiously soothes the heart, ease pain, refresh the mind and provide strength to continue life's journey.

However, poetry is not just a divine utterance. It is the human voice, speaking directly to reassure us of a life that exists beyond mere existence. Poetry is not an ephemeral burst of youthful passion, constrained by age or external forces. Rather, it is a never-ending quest for deeper truths, often hidden from plain sight, that continue to fuel the poet's imagination and spirit.

Thus, a poet is the product of his time. He writes the language of his age, yet poetry does not simply document the political or social events of the moment. Poetry is not a mere vehicle for expressing transient concerns. It lives independently, a force with its own life and direction. Its voice is not just an echo but a powerful entity in its own right: the sentinel of the poet's conscience, the voice of nature, the embodiment of joy and the eternal melody of love, humanity and compassion.

Indeed, translation is not just an academic exercise; it is an act of preserving the poetic grandeur. The poetic sensibilities of the translators shine through the work's spontaneity, precision and the skillful use of literary devices, ensuring that the grandeur of the original is not lost in translation. The language, though simple in its diction, is profound in its impact, inviting readers to reflect upon the layers of meaning entrenched in each line.

The English translation of *Ahalya* of Dr. Phani Mohanty, renowned Odia poet embodies the distilled essence of the poets' personal worlds aligned with the universal. This epic poem is simple yet profound, marked by a purity of language and an admirable clarity of thought. *Ahalya*, intricately weaves together mythology and concealed love themes, resonating with readers on a deeply emotional and intellectual level. Mohanty, the Sahitya Akademi Awardee poet brings forth a poetic vision that captures the timeless nature of his subject matter. His ability to bring the ancient myth of 'Ahalya' to life in a contemporary context speaks to the eternal relevance of such stories, with their capacity to evoke timeless human emotions.

Ahalya translated from Odia to English by Sonali Sahu, a young translator is a significant achievement, one that conveys the lyrical beauty and emotional depth of Mohanty's original work. In the poem, the poetic persona delves into the mythological tale of Ahalya, a character from the Ramayana to explore the deeper themes of human suffering and redemption. Ahalya, cursed by her husband, Sage Gautama is turned to stone for a moment of weakness enduring years of isolation and torment. Mohanty poignantly captures her profound anguish, portraying her as a symbol of human suffering, highlighting the emotional and spiritual pain that often accompanies the consequences of one's actions. He depicts the predicament of his Newfoundland, Ahalya and her intense passion. The pain of her endless waiting is evident in the beginning of the poem.

> No beginning, no end-
> Only ceaseless waiting
> On this desolate land,
>
> *(Ahalya, my translation)*

The poet metaphorically portrays the transformative power of divine intervention. Ahalya's eventual redemption by Lord Rama brings her relief and joy, symbolizing hope and the possibility of renewal for all humankind. Through her story, the poet weaves a narrative of trials, tribulations and the ultimate triumph of grace and salvation offering a reflection on the resilience of the human spirit and the capacity for redemption. Further the poet accentuates the complexities of human nature, the consequences of betrayal, the possibility of redemption and the transformative power of divine mercy. However, the ray of hope and the future of possibilities have been reflected at the end of the poem with the arrival of the Supreme Personality of Virtue. Thus he says

> You are a sanctum of peace,
> Where virtues bloom in tranquil embrace.
> With your arrival,
> My life finds sublime grace.
>
> *(Ahalya, my translation)*

The perspectives offered by the poet are not merely personal; they resonate with universal truths about the human condition touching on themes of love, loss, joy, and quest. This poem stands as a testament to the power of poetry to transcend the limitations of time and space offering readers a glimpse into the hearts and minds of poets from different walks of life.

Ms. Sonali Sahu, the budding translator has embarked on a humble yet remarkable journey of bridging the cultural and linguistic divide by translating the epic of Dr. Phani Mohanty from Odia to English. Through her thoughtful and meticulous translation she has managed to preserve the essence of the original work while making it accessible to a global audience. Sahu's deep appreciation for Odia literature and her linguistic skills shine through her translation offering readers a quick look into the richness of Mohanty's poetry. Her effort is a testament to her passion for literature and her belief in the power of words to transcend boundaries fostering cross-cultural understanding and appreciation.

However, Sahu has approached this task with meticulous care, ensuring that the essence of the original poem remains intact while making it accessible to a wider audience. Her translation is marked by a fluidity and grace that mirrors the tone and rhythm of the original maintaining its lyrical quality despite the challenges posed by the irregular verse forms. The delicate balance between accuracy and creativity in this translation enhances the reader's engagement allowing the universal themes of Ahalya's story to resonate deeply across linguistic boundaries. The care and diligence with which Sahu has undertaken this task is evident and her contribution to bringing Mohanty's work to a wider audience is worthy of admiration.

It is with great hope that this translation of *Ahalya* will not only meet with the approbation of readers but also inspire them to explore the original works of Mohanty. This is a volume that speaks to the timeless relevance of poetry and its ability to capture the essence of human experience making it a significant contribution to the world of literature.

Chittaranjan Bhoi, *MPhil, PhD (Utkal)*
Associate Professor & Dean
School of Comparative Tribal Languages and Literatures
KISS Deemed to be University
Bhubaneswar, Odisha

Translator's Note

Translating Ahalya of Dr. Phani Mohanty was an inexplicable experience for me. This work is not just a retelling of an age-old mythological episode; it is a profound reflection on the sufferings of women across time and space. Ahalya, a significant figure in Hindu mythology, is often remembered for her curse and subsequent redemption by Lord Rama. However, what remains largely unspoken is the injustice she endured—her silent suffering, the lack of agency, and the societal neglect that allowed her pain to continue until divine intervention occurred.

Ahalya: The Silent Victim of a Patriarchal Society

Ahalya, according to mythology, was the wife of Sage Gautama, known for her beauty and wisdom. The story suggests that she was deceived by Indra, the king of gods, who disguised himself as her husband. When Sage Gautama discovered this, he did not seek to understand the situation but instead cursed Ahalya to turn into stone, condemning her to ages of suffering. The most striking part of her tale is that she was punished without committing a mistake. No one questioned the injustice of her fate—neither the sages nor the intellectuals of that time. Her suffering was normalized until Lord Rama arrived in Treta Yuga and liberated her with his divine touch.

Dr. Phani Mohanty, through his poetic and thought-provoking writing, compels us to reconsider Ahalya's story beyond its mythological context. He raises significant questions: If Ahalya was innocent, why was she cursed? Why was Indra, the actual deceiver, not held accountable? Why did society remain silent in the face of such an injustice? These questions are not merely relevant to ancient times but continue to resonate in the modern world.

Relevance of Ahalya's Story in Contemporary Society:

Even today, women across the world find themselves in situations similar to Ahalya's. They suffer injustice, discrimination, and oppression, often without any fault of their own. They are judged, silenced, and made to bear the brunt of patriarchal norms. Whether it is domestic violence, workplace harassment, social stigma, or honor killings, the oppression of women remains a harsh reality.

Dr. Mohanty's Ahalya is not just a poem; it is a mirror to society. It forces us to acknowledge that while ages have passed, the fundamental treatment of women has not changed much. In today's world, women still wait for their metaphorical 'Rama'—a savior who will recognize their pain and restore their dignity. But the real question remains: Why do women still need a savior? Why can't society itself rise to protect, support, and stand for them?

Challenges and Emotional Depth in Translating Ahalya:

Translating Ahalya was not just a literary task; it was an emotional and intellectual journey. The depth of Dr. Mohanty's words, the intensity of his emotions, and the weight of his questions made the process both challenging and enlightening. One of the primary challenges was retaining the poetic essence while ensuring that the deeper meanings were not lost. His work is rich with metaphors and layered with philosophical undertones. As a translator, my responsibility was to carry the soul of his writing into another language without distorting its impact. I had to ensure that the readers could feel the same anguish, the same questions, and the same urgency that Dr. Mohanty intended to convey.

Another challenge was the cultural context. Ahalya is deeply rooted in Indian mythology, and while the story is universally powerful, some references needed to be made accessible to a wider audience. At the same time, I had to be careful not to over-explain, as that would dilute the strength of the narrative. Balancing cultural authenticity with readability was a crucial part of the translation process.

Why Ahalya's Story Must Be Retold:

Ahalya's story is not just about mythology; it is about every woman who has suffered in silence. It is about every voice that was suppressed, every injustice that was ignored, and every pain that was normalized. By translating Ahalya, I felt a deep responsibility to bring this powerful narrative to more readers, to spark conversations, and to remind society of the urgent need for change. Dr. Phani Mohanty's work is a call to action. It urges us to break the silence, to challenge the norms, and to create a better world for women.

However, I must mention that translating this great work into English came with its own set of challenges. The poem contains intricate references to Indian mythology and Sanskrit words, along with high-level metaphors and imagery. Despite these hurdles, I tried my level best to remain true to the original poem, capturing its essence without distorting its meaning. The task was to retain the beauty and emotional depth of the original Odia poem, ensuring that the lyrical flow and cultural nuances were preserved in the translation. While I have made every effort to keep the work as authentic as possible, I leave it to my readers to decide how they perceive my translation.

-1-

No beginning, no end—
Only ceaseless waiting
On this desolate land,
Stretching into infinity.
Like a stormy sky,
That wreaks ruin in its wake,
This waiting becomes
A searing death within life.

On sorrow's swing,
Desire sways—
Caught adrift between life and afterlife.
Unyielding, ruthless destiny
Unfolds upon time's fragile fabric,
Suspended,
Dripping like dew
From desolate leaves.

Night dons a veil of dew,
A deep, hushed silence
Wraps the world
In the sullen, wordless dawn
Of the forest.
A distant cottage glimmers,
A morning star in the dim light—
Once a revered shrine,
Imbued with purity and love,
A realm of exalted ideals
For the holy *Aryavarta*.

History offers fleeting glimpses
Of an eternal age,
Weaving a tale of love,
Memory, and forgetfulness,
Threaded with the ephemeral echoes
Of bygone events.
History, a ruthless sovereign,
Remains unyielding, indifferent,
Starkly merciless.
From the grim depths of yesterday,
It breathes life into tales,
Adorning them with masks.
Of varied fates and roles,
Both grand and humble,
From veins of intertwined destinies,

History nurtures a child,
Whose lifeblood bears
The finest gifts of epochs to come.
Upon their brow,
The sacred sandalwood marks
Are shadowed by cruelty—
Hatred, envy, and disgrace—
Softened only by the gentle
Caress of destiny's grace.

Amid the infinite expanse
Of mortal strife on this Earth,
Where sorrow and suffering
Merge with fear and desolation,
A relentless dance unfolds—
Weariness and decay intertwined.
Life, a blend of joy and sorrow,

Like a frail boat trembling
In the turbulent embrace
Of a roaring river.
What was once
My heart's deepest treasure,
Intimately mine,
Drifts into the vast unknown.

Day by day, the forsaken,
Lifeless Earth wanders the void,
While the somber blue sky,
A tender, pure, pristine zone,
Of a living statue of love,
Stretching wide,
A veil of earthly compassion.
Sorrowful, yet endlessly tranquil,
It cradles the world with quiet grace—
An eternal sanctuary,
Whispering of solace and infinite care.

-2-

The scheming, lingering threads of time,
Carelessly scattering
Fistfuls of mossy forgetfulness
Across the auspicious moments
Of early Asadha.
In the dreamy, exuberant Siddhashrama,
Sages and scholars—
Immersed in eloquent deliberation,
Articulate contemplation—
Wove tapestries of discourse:
Concrete, dexterous, masculine,
And unfathomably vast.

Amid dense, cloud-laden skies,
Caught in an unresolved conflict,
The flame of selfishness ignites
Within the goddess's heart—
A blaze of consciousness, set apart.
In the groaning conspiracy,
Like ghosts haunting barren fields,
Goutam's sorrowful smile emerges—
Alone, poignant, enduring.
Then suddenly, an unforeseen event,
A fearless, serene voice breaks through,
Simple yet profound.
Within the bustling ashram's expanse,
A silent seeker stands,
A living statue in trance.

Under the spell of inevitable decline,
Gripped by the hands of unyielding decay,
Echoes of wisdom in meditation shine,
While righteousness awaits a dawning day.
Before our eyes, a colony reawakes,
Entangled in a silken trap's cruel sway,
Traditions virtuous, emotions unspoken,
Clashing to forge their ultimate way.
A symphony of conspiracy unfolds,
In adversaries' intricate, chaotic dance.
Serene amidst the storm's fierce blaze,
Gautam rose in unforeseen circumstance.
On a revolution's unstable earthly stage,
The narrative turns a poet, wise and sage.
In tranquil dreams, where blue shades emerge,
Worn and weathered, lies a tale unsung—its verge.

From infinite void to wisdom's soaring height,
In the poet's realm, where dreams ignite,
Born of the depths of an ultimate quest,
A timeless tale finds eternal rest.
History gleams, polished bright and clear,
Shining forth with a radiant sphere,
Draped in flesh, a luminous cloak,
Guiding through fate, its path bespoke.

No remedy for events
That slipped away,
No force in reality can contend
With pride's ascend, arrogant and unbent.
In the tyrant's domain,
Unchecked, grand,

Questions of restraint
Simply disband.
Beneath dark clouds of sorrow,
Once-bright skies wane.
Silent torment grips, uncertain,
Framed by pale faces,
As discipline wanes.
Traditions falter,
Virtues retreat,
Ideals unravel
In their defeat.

To tremble before death's shroud—
Utter foolishness.
A tragedy strikes the court,
Terrifying with final breath.
Like wounded soldiers,
Wounded I stand,
Triumphant, yet weary
From life's relentless hand.
Amidst the unknown,
In doubt's disarray,
Each moment etched
With tears that flow, unseen,
From eyes that bear the weight
Of battles won, yet woe.
Beside cascades of tears,
Where illusions meet the mundane,
In the abyss of uncertainty,
Amidst demonic forces,
Roam fearless wanderers.

-3-

How toneless that moment was,
Indelibly inauspicious,
When your flying chariot,
Adorned with divine flowers
And glittering gems,
Landed abruptly, yet deliberately—
On the chest of my beautiful world,
Shamelessly, without consent.
Your arrival,
Like an elegant emperor
Of an imperial court,
Unwelcome and unasked for,
Cast a pall all around—
Pathetic, inevitable.
My misfortune, my sorrow.

How helpless I was,
No light left in my life.
Days faded away—
Night after night,
Darker, ruinous.
I am dying in the squeal of hell,
Too unbearable.
The whole cosmos
Seems fused with my screaming.
My ruthless fate,
A lifeless life,
Drowned in pain,
Piteous and forlorn.
Once, I was so happy—

Not just happy,
But the happiest.
Purely naïve,
Exceptionally sincere,
In splendid isolation.
I dwelled in seclusion
With my living God,
Cheerfully flying
Through my colourful skies,
Desireless and distant
From aspirations.
Not even thirsty
For an affluent paradise.
But then,
Mysterious silence arrived,
Burning me,
Melting my soft heart
In the searing heat
Of infinite warmth.

Like an imprisoned bird
In a confined cage,
I am tied cruelly
To an illustrated globe,
Boundless and unending.
As long as life lives in me,
My own reflection
Will writhe and squirm like
A snake, partially dead.
These countless nights
Will pass in grief,
Waves of pain drowning
My innocent eyes.

As clouds gather,
They will break
Ripple after ripple
Beneath the amber sky,
A storm of sorrow.

I am restless, helpless,
My pain ebbs day by day,
Growing unknown
Amid familiar faces.
In this vast world,
Humiliated, hostile,
In endless agony—
Disgracefully cast adrift.
Slowly, this wretched fate of mine
Will be erased completely,
Scattered from the golden pages of history—
Like a withered leaf,
Fallen from an ancient tree.

-4-

This ashen time looms grimly,
My life, dejected and sorrowful,
Suspended in a vast void.
The plight of women—a flickering lamp,
Unstable, burdened, I carry this anguish,
Striving to survive
Through endless, unyielding despair.
Caught in war's relentless grip,
My heart and mind are wounded,
Entangled in the ceaseless battle
Of vices and virtues.
So painfully, I feel lost.

These eyes, numb and clogged,
Resist both opening and closing,
Haunted by the piercing gaze of that monster,
Scattering my thoughts.
I exist, broken—
Not for extinction, but for survival.
My being spreads, fragmented,
An echo of that shameful moment.
My heart weeps,
And this body—
Cursed, lamentable,
As pitiful as a grieving widow,
Pristine and newly scarred,
Encircled in the mysterious geometry
Of an endless loop,
Returning, again and again,
To its origin.

Time apathetically flows,
But my thoughts remain numb,
Withering before they bloom,
Akin to a bud denied the sun.
Like a lifeless rat,
Both my aching existence
And I lie trapped in the snares of fate.
Above it all, the sun departs,
Leaving me in shadow,
Devoid of hope.

Distant fade the charms of colors,
Sound's vibrancy lost to my deafened world.
The songs of returning birds,
The cascade's gentle splash—
All melodies fall silent to my ears.
My eyes, wide open yet unseeing,
And this heart, pounding in wary rhythm,
Cling to solitude's cold embrace.
Life drags itself forward,
While death treads ever closer,
 Its discordant echoes resonating
All around.

-5-

In an ill-fated moment,
I find myself adrift,
Like a wrecked log
Lying joyless and forlorn
Amidst the tempest of fear and anxiety.
Seeking no sympathy,
I choose to endure,
To live this solitary life,
Till the debt I owe
Is fully repaid.

Like a tattered flag
After a calamitous storm,
My mind writhes in anguish.
And from the distant, cloudless sky,
Endless thunder resounds,
Its arrogant silence
Shattering the fragile dreamscape
I once held dear.
Now, as the threads of this imagined world
Unravel before me,
Even the three realms tremble,
Their fleeting joys
No more than echoes, fading..
Somehow.

So much has come to pass,
Yet not a single pious soul
Dared to stand firm beside me.
The ascetics, sages, monks,

Guests, and celibates—
Each chose their solitary path,
Pointing fingers at me,
Accusing me of shattering
The sanctity of their hermitage.
They stood silent,
Like prisoners convicted,
Unwilling to confront
The raw and stark truth:
The unbearable torment
Inflicted upon
A helpless woman.

-6-

In my anguish,
I radiate with an unyielding glow,
A fervent ardor burns within,
Thirsting for love's tender embrace.
I shine like a beacon, luminous and true,
Bright and virtuous,
The golden flame gleams, eternal and bold.
Grace and elegance define my form,
My waist, so fair and fine,
A beauty surpassing the divine.
Yet with each passing day,
My strength begins to wane.
The essence of this noble,
Disciplined life—
Is woven in the fabric of time,
Moment by moment,
Fleeting ceaselessly.

What is truth?
What is the divine assurance of protection?
What embodies the essence of moral ideals?
Definitions elude, too strange to grasp,
None holds the answers.
Adrift in sobriety,
Lingering questions sift
Through hearts, unresolved.
Into the abyss of 'truth,' I sank,
Witnessing power's misuse—
As if ensnared
By the cosmic night's embrace,

Amidst the gloom,
No trace of light.

Adrift, without a trail to tread,
A blind soul, lost in a realm of dilemma,
Unseen by the world's splendor,
Stranded in plight.
Like the ancient bow of Shiva,
Forgotten, cast in an abandoned room—
Bound by a silent vow,
Caught in someone's distant gaze,
Lying dejectedly, shrouded in stillness.
Yet I knew—
Promises do not speak,
They do not engage in dialogue.
Silent witnesses to the ceaseless flow of time,
They endure,
Bearing the weight of ages upon ages.

What fate is mine,
To don the mask of life's performance,
Pretending, endlessly pretending,
Before disinterested eyes,
Time and time again.
On this vacant stage,
No tongue in any lexicon
Can narrate the plight of my soul.
Words of wisdom slip
Through my grasp—
Like floating garlands of clouds
On an infinite horizon.
No matter how fiercely I try to hold on,
My shattered self resists,

Unready, unwilling
To be pieced together once more.
Endless silence blankets the suppressed earth,
Ruling like a solitary star—
Creating itself, expanding its reach,
Yet decomposing, moment by fleeting moment.
A man, steeped in dejection,
Waits quietly in the shadow of society,
Yearning for its sanction,
With the greatest, most unyielding affection.

From what marvelous element
Was Ahalya so wondrously fashioned?
This body, of blood and flesh,
Is beautifully shaped, a divine impression.
From which distant realm of dreams
Does your eternal voice softly resonate, Ahalya?
You are the companion on the journey,
Transforming tender emotions into love,
Manifesting extraordinary expressions
Of boundless empathy.
Oh, divine embodiment of love!
In the realm of verses, you stand sublime—
A creation of celestial wonder.
In every echo,
A melody resounds,
Of unparalleled sensation.

-7-

After the catastrophe,
The sky shattered,
Descending upon the Earth's chest
With a mighty roar,
Like the severed head of a fallen Titan.
The Earth cleaved in two,
And in the blink of an eye,
A deluge of destruction
Split the land into nine realms.
Darkness gripped every direction,
Profound gloom enveloped all.
From the silence emerged
A child of time,
Crying like a newborn,
Beneath the ominous gaze
Of brooding clouds.

Sorrow encircled me,
Ahalya—fragile emblem of suffering's touch—
Unafraid, resolute in duty's call,
An ever-watchful sentinel,
Ensnared in time's relentless wheel.
Besieged, she wanders adrift,
Lost in shadowed plight,
Drawn to the allure
Of unseen demonic power.
Captivated, she dwells
In her humble abode,
Enraptured,
Lost in contemplative fire.

Embraced by the mystery
Of an unfamiliar touch,
In the brutality of relentless caress,
It feels, at times,
Like being engulfed
In the forceful embrace of demonic kisses.
For a fleeting moment,
It feels like calling it her own.

Yet, to close her eyes,
To not meet the gaze,
Feels strange today.
Remembered words slip
From the heart,
The stranger's touch
Creeps through her,
Spreading like shadows.
In the bare darkness,
A body aglow,
Like moonlit flair.
Two forms,
Shrinking and shifting,
On the silent Earth's heart.
Ahalya, engrossed in the erotic sense,
Wanders within herself,
Lost, with no discernible path.

In a moment's sweat,
The struggle undoes all.
Ornaments scatter bitterly,
Her expression remains elusive.
Hair, shattered like dark clouds,
Falls with each breath and sigh.

A sinful soul rises,
Like a wounded wrestler,
Like a sailor of a broken boat.
With large, searching eyes,
And a heavy heart,
She silences herself,
Mending the pieces
Of her unfortunate fate.

In the quest for life's full embrace,
Fearing death's shadow,
The body's grace fades.
With each passing day,
Strength wanes,
Life's essence drains.
Like the extinguished flame
Of a forgotten lamp,
In the depths of oblivion's game,
No one sees—
Neither loss nor gain—
Through love's decree.
In joys and sorrows,
Side by side we yearn,
Yet companionship remains elusive.

Ahalya, alive or deceased,
Knows not her fate.
No remedy is released.
Innocent as Ganga's pure flow,
She accepts her destined role,
Without guilt's shadow,
Bearing the weight Of untold trials.
Her wise soul's journey,

Adorned with cunning boldness,
Fights battles unspoken—
Without treaties signed,
Without documents penned.
Fierce wars rage
Within the conscious mind.

Beneath her feet,
The Earth burns.
In the pot of shame,
Flames burst in fiery haze.
From the crimson sky,
Stones rain down.
Ahalya floats against Yamuna's stream,
Each feather of time's golden wing
Falling gracefully,
One by one.

-8-

In the wet house,
Draped as a *yogini*,
I sit in serenity,
Chanting softly with my rosary.
Oh God, my humble prayer:
May the life I lived,
Burdened with sacrifices,
Never repeat itself
In another woman's destiny.
Whether I exist or not,
It matters little;
My destiny is blind,
Devoid of desires or action.
Years will pass,
A silent yearning lingering
For inevitable liberation.
Yet I know too well—
Liberation is never easy
In this life of bondage.

To endure the world's suffering,
Its constant fear and insecurity,
Born of sin, Is to walk among fiery embers
Of remorse.
An innocent child turns to ash,
And my life stumbles forward,
Treading painfully
On the stones of regret.

"Fate's" door,
Whether of fortune or despair,
Remains closed to me still.
Restlessly I linger,
Awaiting someone's promise
With fervent hope.
In hushed, wordless silence,
Amid the anciently cursed,
In these enchanting, unfinished woods,
History has wandered,
Void of boundaries,
Within the delicate beauty of society.
In imagined horror,
An unforeseen, terrifying regime
Startles this beautiful world.

Injustice and disdain
Grasp it tightly.
From rebellion's fiery forge,
Revolutionaries emerge.
Blazing in fury,
They devastate the golden future.
Lamentation echoes endlessly,
As sorrow bleeds
In the arena of strife.

Yet a fresh saga shall rise—
Through the tumult's rush,
Waves rise and fall,
Shaping and breaking
The ocean of consciousness.
In meaningless verses,
I lay bare my proof:

Social innocence stained
By the weight of sin.
Like a tree heavy with ripe fruits,
I remain grounded on this Earth,
Ready to fall at last.

Through years of experience,
Ancient societies faltered—
Inadequate stewards of justice and revolution.
Today, the sky of possibilities
Lies obscured and murky.
This life,
Plagued by affliction and suffering,
Fades each day Into the hymn of time.

-9-

Allow me, my dear,
This final departure.
This preciously unlucky life
Has ebbed in vain,
A fleeting game of hide-and-seek
With the gloaming shadows.
Indeed, this life—
Bound by rules and practices
Drawn by these social beings—
Holds me captive.
Yet death is not for the soul,
But for this unfortunate,
Eternal body.

What wretched fate is mine?
Feeble and helpless I remain,
Even with a pious,
Innocent soulmate beside me.
Miserably alone,
Like a cow separated from its herd,
I endure the weal and woe
Of this widowed existence.
Profit, loss, pain, and delight,
For me, are alike—
Drops of dew
On brittle weeds,
Glittering and fleeting
In the early November morning.

How unfortunate I am,
Though cloaked,
Safe and unharmed,
Yet bound to die silently,
Wrapped in acute suffering.
There may be no time
To repent.
Let my impure body
Rest upon a floral bed,
Touched by your tender love,
With all its pleasure.
Let me dissolve Into the boundless blue—
The rhythm of absolute silence.

Listen, my beloved,
Even with the melody of joy
In the faraway sky,
Even amidst the omnivorous flames
Of an untended graveyard,
You remain my most cherished one.
Oh, my darling! Though glee and joy
Linger near my grasp,
They slip away,
Eluding my bounds.
Like an unstable boat
In the middle of a restless river,
This woeful life
Fractures time and again,
Breaking meaninglessly.
Now the final curtain draws near,
Closing on tender thoughts,
Love, and relief.
Despite my fragile health,

My unsteady mind,
And grave anguish, I shall wait,
Like an untethered yogini,
Hoping for recognition,
Dreaming of respect—
Until eternity.

The hallowed hours of waiting,
Whiffs of sandalwood's embrace,
Carried gently on the breeze,
Whispering secrets of distant grace.
A heavenly soul will appear,
Gracefully,
From an unseen realm,
With the chiming tones
Of a celestial anklet—
Banishing the curse
Of my life.

-10-

Who are you,
The supremely blessed soul of divine grace?
In the luminous wonder
Of which celestial marvel
Is your radiant abode?
Amidst the fiery core of revolution,
What bond does your unyielding spirit share
With this oppressed woman?
Connection—
A line drawn on water,
Ephemeral and fleeting.
With love comes betrayal,
With life, its shadow—death.
Joy entwines with sorrow,
As honor mingles with disdain.

-11-

Like an uninvited, unwelcomed guest,
You appeared suddenly,
Emerging from the vast sky,
Turning my darkly adorned land
Into desolation.
The tender bird of love
Was seized by strong, merciless claws,
Its tiny eyes glimpsing a fixed fate—
A future of unknown plants and stars,
Trembling in the shadow
Of inevitable death.

Is death the destiny
Of the suffering or the oppressor?
The sinner or the memory-torn mind?
The trembling body?
Or is it the conclusion
Of meaningless silence?"

I became a stranger to myself
After that catastrophe.
In distant shores of ceaseless strife,
Fear and guilt, like heavy clouds,
Obscure my dreams.
My distant voyage unfolds,
A quest to transcend the burdens
Of this frail, ever-changing body.
In the tranquil depths of azure eyes,
Waves of sorrow gently rise,

Carrying their burdens silently
Across the vast inner seas.
Through the relentless sparks of retribution,
The indomitable mind wearily endures.
Yet many efforts to forget
Prove futile.

The painful scene etches itself
Repeatedly before my eyes,
Like a brand seared into the heart.
With every attempt to erase it,
The tyrant's relentless dance echoes,
Reverberating with the unforgettable anguish
Of that timeless moment's trance.

In the eternal inquiry of life and death,
The heart withdraws, aloof.
In the mime of passive indifference,
There dwells a silent defiance.
Where values and ideals fade,
Betrayed by the silent charade,
This anguish lingers—
A melody of sorrow,
Unyielding and profound.

-12-

Burdened by the void of her being,
She bears the weight of imposed sorrow,
The stain of disgrace cloaked
In quiet grace.
Bound by the chains of duty,
She braves the dense fog
Of censure and shame.
Amid the ceaseless battle
Of meaningless silence,
The helpless noble woman
Exists as a stranger to herself.
Silent through the ages,
She shares the sorrow
Of the compassionate,
Waiting for someone to arrive—
Someone who truly understands
Her pain.

What kind of life is this, oh God?
Beloved companion, dearest friends,
Cherished son, familiar faces—
None to be found,
No one close in the distant future.
Even knowing this,
In the timeless anticipation of reunion,
Through cycles of birth and rebirth,
She lies in the ancient fortress of ego,
Amidst the unbroken waves of desire.
Her mountain of patience
Quakes, fractured like stone.

In an unknown, mysterious cycle,
Her existence dissolves into
A mere shadow.

Events spiral beyond her grasp—
Union, separation, renunciation,
All rendered meaningless.
She dwells in full emptiness,
A tranquil sky
Where waves dare not swell,
Where the touch of blood
Carries no tale to tell.
From within and without,
Each moment blooms
With fearsome rebellion.
Uncounted through ages untold,
She rests akin to Mother Earth—
An icon of forgiveness,
A sculpture of compassion.

Omit history's tears for her plight,
But spare her the weight of sympathy
In poetic light.
Amidst yogic solitude,
She seeks tranquil stillness,
Where souls can confide.
Until every moment merges seamlessly,
Let her rest in the uncharted expanse
Of profound emptiness.
Her existence burns perpetually,
Lost in the twilight of societal norms,
Where shadows of ignorance prevail—
A dim, murky light

Guided by an unseen, tainted hand.
Her heart remains profoundly melancholic,
Submerged in sorrow's river.
Her life, tarnished yet serene,
Gentle, and bittersweet.

Amid death's tender embrace,
Women surrender to the extremity
Of their era—
A painful blaze of wonder,
A life perpetually unsettled.
In the fearful reverence of faith
Amid crisis, She is an offering—
A symbol of fear and awe.
In the golden land of falsehood's
Unyielding creation,
Profound mystery lies concealed
Under the cloak of darkness.

In the gentle, soft touch of someone,
Dormant energy awakens,
Unleashing a blissful creativity
That lingers as eternal memory.
In the celebration of tradition,
An innocent, enraptured mind
Surrenders in deep gratitude—
A life incomplete, yet whole.

-13-

In the melancholy silence
Of an entrancing melody,
The routine of ordinary life unravels.
On the wings of a sorrowful night,
A loveless sensation wanders aimlessly,
Seeking vivid refuge.
A graceful, tender form,
With large, restless eyes,
Adorned in an enchanting radiance—
Pure and sparkling like a diamond—
Sweet, luminous.

In the sway of the breeze,
In the allure of gentle touch,
In the longing of an intense embrace,
In the fierce tenderness of kisses,
She offers her body with steadfast resolve,
Free of judgment,
Discerning neither fault nor virtue.
Friendless and adrift,
The empty world knows no solace.
Beyond sin and virtue,
A strong, robust form
Unites with a tender one,
Blending into solitary oneness.

Through the eyelids, vivid scenes emerge—
Terrifying visions of weapons
Unfold across the mind's canvas.
The seven seas churn with tumultuous upheaval,

Swirling in chaos,
Like an ancient python—
Coiled and restless.
Without the thunderous roar of clouds,
Or the fiery strike of lightning,
The vast sky echoes
The trumpet of cosmic dissolution.
An ominous portent,
Meticulously winged and feminine,
Meets an untimely demise.

Amid the dense cascade of dark shadows,
Life's belief in death falters.
In the blink of an eye,
Day and night blur—
Traditions, pride,
And the hues of family honour
Veil the tarnished portrait of life.
Once radiant,
A graceful lineage crumbles
To dust and ashes,
Returning,
Silent, to the earth.

-14-

The mortal body is lying alone
On the earth,
Imprisoned in grief in its own home.
Forgive me unintended errors
With the gentle veil
Of your pure compassion,
Wipe away the tears kindly,
Give me a final kiss
In a profound embrace.

In the place of sorrow and suffering
I am imprisoned for life,
Today, my state is like a dewdrop
Shattered by a wave,
Upon someone's gesture,
I repeatedly fall into aimless thoughts
Like a puppet rising and falling
Performing a new act.

No hopeful expectations, no shores to bind,
Life's dreamlike edges, elusive to find,
Narrating playful moments,
In words so frail,
Capturing life's essence,
A fleeting tale,
The innate tenderness of touch,
Now lost,
In the sea of nerves,
The same note and thrill
No longer exist.

From any of the flute's holes,
No enchanting melody springs forth,
If life still dwells within this body
I lack the courage to discern.

Countless memories entwined
On the veil of a fading gaze.

From the moving pictures they arise,
From some unknown, inner skies,
The dreadful roar of cosmic doom,
Echoes through the looming gloom.

In the silence of seven realms,
The flute's anxious song resounds,
In the azure sky, the sweet vibration
Of the mad wind,
Like one hundred sons of the blind king,
The radiant clusters of profound wisdom,
Resonate in every particle of the universe,
Echoing the cries of pain.
In this dilapidated abode of dreams,
Day and night, my heart is torn apart,
Tearful cries, moments steeped
In thrilling memories.

For the atonement of the sins I have committed,
Like the sage, I stand forever
Caught in the flame of self-exploration,
In a corrupt hermitage of my own making.

Where, in the vastness of my solitude,
I embraced life with humility,
Carrying the weight of countless moments ,
In silence, I remained.

Until the stained body shed its shame,
And in the purity of spirit, untainted,
I wandered through the nectar of truth,
Untouched, unbroken by the burdens of the past.

-15-

In the tender, delicate touch of another
My slumber broke, swift and sudden,
In the rustling leaves, in the blooming flowers,
In the flames of the pyre,
In the sacred utterances,
As clouds wandered above,
A soft rain of nectar poured down,
In the gentle, shimmering embrace of the divine.

O my eternal companion of lifetimes,
You come as a sweet, fragrant essence,
As a melody so tender, so sweet,
As the moon's soft glow,
You arrive.
You make me free of ego,
Lifting me up,
Filling me with joy,
Awakening wonder,
Leaving me entranced and amazed,
In the divine nectar of bliss.

You descend from the endless sky,
On a chariot, untouched and pure,
Transforming the forsaken, hollowed ground
Into a garland of blossoms, rich and divine.
On a moonless, starry night,
You arrive,

A lotus of love and compassion,
Blooming in the withered ruins of my life,
Bringing grace, rebirth and the dawn of hope.

In the soft hues of your form, on gentle feet,
The shimmering anklets of diamonds dance,
A tale of longing woven in jasmine's breath,
A melody deep, with a sorrowful grace.

On the wings of clouds, with a tender touch,
The veil of compassion and forgiveness flows,
O my eternal dream, my long-lost beloved!

In dust, in forgotten realms, in boundless worlds,
Your voice calls, a melody soft and sweet,
As rain pours on a chariot of joy,
Bathing me in the coolness of purity,
In the dense, fragrant groves of longing,
In the southern breeze, so soft and wild,
In the maddening whispers of the tender wind,
You arrive,
Touching, inhaling,
Purifying every impure limb and courtyard,
Awakening the subtle essence of every being,
Enchanting my troubled, restless soul
With the sacred spell of your love.

In the dense curls of the monsoon clouds,
The gentle stream of rain falls,
As the evening sky glows with the crimson hue,
A shimmering, celestial star emerges.
In the longing, I drift in the endless blue ocean,
Amidst the murky darkness,

Where the restless song of desire
Echoes through the night's sorrowful tune.
Far beyond, where shadows meet the sun,
You stand,
With the dark flute of love's silent call,
Under the gentle moon's soft glow,
A melody of longing stirs within you.

In the fearless gesture of your form,
You draw near,
And my being, ablaze with your tender love,
Finds your embrace spreading across the endless sky,
In dreams and memories,
O *Astama Rudra* !
Defying the laws of fate,
I am lost in your glory,
Drowned in the awe
Of your eternal magnificence.

-16-

Like an angel, gentle as moonlight
In the quiet embrace of night,
From what distant cosmos
Did you silently descend,
Divine and ethereal,
Stepping softly into my life?
You illuminated my disarrayed hair
With shimmering stars of silver,
Floating freely in the river's embrace.
Standing still for a fleeting moment
Amid the irregular darkness of the house,
In the tender language of silence,
You whispered like a honeybee,
Awakening depths unknown.
In the blink of an eye,
Tears held back began to fall,
From ankle to the tips of my hair,
Each drop a gentle cascade.

In the tenderness of your touch,
I forgot myself entirely.
You spoke of the ultimate fulfillment—
Unblemished destiny in patience,
Serenity, goodness, and cherished desire.
Oh goddess of faith, wisdom, and devotion,
Oh radiant one!
Far beyond my mortal aspirations,
In the marble glow of the forest grove,
In the whispers carried by the breeze,
In the extraordinary valor of

Dawn's Vaisakhi hymn,
You shine brighter still.

With hair adorned by celestial blue,
You embody a hymn adrift in the air.
In the council's poised gesture,
You shimmer divine—
A heavenly realm in a pilgrim's delight.
Like the sacred Ganges flowing
From hallowed *Gangotri*,
Pure and abundant,
You navigate with grace.
Like the eternal flow of time,
Endlessly joyous,
Fulfilling the essence
Of a richly flowing life.

-17-

In the charm of your tender words,
In the enchanting sweetness
Of your captivated-like form,
I am suddenly lost—
Adrift in the melody of my existence.
Like a thunderbolt,
Your support transformed
My frail muscles and bones—
Strengthened, resolute.
Within the weight of my thoughts,
You floated gracefully,
Light as clouds gathering on the horizon.
Surprised, astonished,
In the stillness of my mind,
Consciousness emerges amidst the darkness,
Invisible, yet deeply felt.

In the blink of my eyes,
Your sacred touch illuminates my being.
After the intoxicating sweetness
Of solitude's sublime charm, I realize—
I am not Another essential, worshipping yogini.
I am Ahalya— Much spoken of in lore,
Yet only an ordinary woman,
Bound by society's chains.
For ages, through countless epochs,
I have been entwined
In the cage of hopeful expectations,
Living a life disguised
As an unanswered question.

A name on the lips of many,
Lost in the dense, dark greenery
Of mystical secrets.
Amidst the play of sunlight and shadow,
Your hidden charms reveal themselves.
The endless sorrow of grieving life fades,
Soothed by cupid's intoxicating beauty.

Like a dream's vivid depiction,
Moments before it breaks,
The monsoon cascades
In rhythmic, dark-blue torrents,
Drenching the skies.
Two sprouting eyes create
A labyrinth of light,
Adorned with the eternal Swastika.
Penetrating the mind's depths,
They bestow profound wisdom.
You are the completeness of life,
The peace my desires seek.
You are the wondrous realization
Of my boundless solitude,
The luminous future
Of infinite possibilities.

You are the sacred experience—
A recital of *Gita*'s purest song,
The gentle melody
Of my sublime aspirations.
Oh, cherished treasure of my heart!
Embrace my flaws, my imperfections,
With your divine blessings.
Electrify my soul In the rumble of new clouds.

Guide me to bow in reverence
To boundless compassion.

In the languid embrace of the night's breeze,
Let no fear disturb my tranquil ease.
Through the ambrosial elixir
Of your embrace, I am enraptured,
Lost in blissful pursuit.
You are my end,
My life's eternal grace.
In my small universe,
Your tender, dark embrace
Shines as my destiny's lasting grace.
In my azure blood flows the awe
Of centuries yet to come.

In the quiet rhythm of dust and smoke,
You are the solemn hymn
Clothing sorrow.
Don't show me pity—
I am but a captive
Of fleeting time's city,
And in your boundless abyss,
I find my sanctuary.

-18-

I will remain bound forever
In the honeyed garden of your love—
Love, untouched by love itself.
Sorrow shall not endure,
Its ephemeral breeze shall pass,
Regret shall not linger,
Nor doubt arise.
Unrest shall not bloom,
No turmoil, no pain,
No sighs cast in vain.

In the gentle, scented breeze of night,
The soul ascends,
Leaving the body's plight.
Freed from bondage,
Through rigorous penance,
Awake to consciousness as Ahalya—
She beholds the vision
In the vast expanse
Of the great cremation ground.

At your arrival,
On the subtle plane of the subconscious,
Gentle tremors ripple.
Amidst blossoms' delicate weight,
In the Jasmine vine's bending grace,
Your final trace remains.
Through restless touch,
Waves of joy rise and surge.
In the irresistible allure

Of a form more beautiful than dreams,
My ancient heart flutters sweetly
In the new cloud of love.
Your enchanting touch,
Like Yashoda's gentle embrace,
Your face, a saintly visage,
Pure and serene,
Radiates grace akin to
The devotion of *Bhagabata*.

-19-

In the spell of intoxication's allure,
Life becomes the fervent longing
Of this pure heart.
Meanings dissipate,
Empty whispers echo in the void.
My finite form,
Immersed in life's profound definitions,
Quivers like a leaf
In the tender breeze—
An eternal, restless mind.
In the play of light,
Like the fleeting gaze of a deer,
In the twilight blue
Of your compassionate embrace,
Spreading across the vast, endless skies,
Oh lotus-born, your grace unfolds.
In twilight's tender caress,

Through your divine, healing touch,
Years of rigidity dissolve,
Leaving emptiness in their wake.
My awareness awakens,
Shedding the veil of confusion.

-20-

Like a blue sky
In the unfortunate skies of sorrow,
You arrive freely,
In your peace, high above,
Like a seamless guest
At an unscheduled hour.
In the divine flute's lofty tune,
As water soothes the pond's lagoon,
I flutter near, fish-like,
In a playful spree.
With steadfast hands,
You have imparted
Countless teachings on fear,
Gracefully dissolving its grip.
Years of collective sorrow, bound,
Transform through turbulent metamorphosis.

The rigidity of body and mind
Softens, flows away,
Leaving stillness.
My enchanted eyes awaken,
Surprised,
As my own voice becomes
Unfamiliar to my distant ears.
At your arrival,
The abandoned ashram's skies
Breathe life anew.

Your presence rekindles

Vitality in every living essence,
Infusing each life
With fresh joy and profound experience.
Oh revered master!
Your unfailing blessings
Are my ultimate treasure,
Illuminating the eternal, cherished life I lead.
Radiant beams perpetually shine,
And in the enigmatic blue
Of monsoon's reign,
Wisdom resides—timeless,
Untouched by age or vanity.

-21-

Truly, your fierce stream of light—
The fleeting stars of nectarous night—
Bloom for but a moment,
Then fade into the vast
Blue expanse of evening sky.

In the resolute woman,
Where weakness finds no place,
I am but a captive bird,
Nestled in the azure folds
Of your tranquil evening veil.
Oh pure and radiant saint,
Embody me with fearlessness—
Empower me, assure me,
Through your gesture of divine courage.

Amidst the glow of radiant dawn,
You transcend ancient realms,
Timeless, flowing in essence eternal.
You are a sanctum of peace,
Where virtues bloom In tranquil embrace.
With your arrival,
My life finds sublime grace.
 In your presence,
Each moment holds its perfect place.
From completeness arises completeness.
When completeness is drawn from completeness,
What remains Is completeness eternal,
A fullness forever replete.

Black Eagle Books

www.blackeaglebooks.org
info@blackeaglebooks.org

Black Eagle Books, an independent publisher, was founded as a nonprofit organization in April, 2019. It is our mission to connect and engage the Indian diaspora and the world at large with the best of works of world literature published on a collaborative platform, with special emphasis on foregrounding Contemporary Classics and New Writing.

www.ingramcontent.com/pod-product-compliance
Lightning Source LLC
Chambersburg PA
CBHW030535080526
44585CB00014B/952